Heart-felt dogs

The canines behind the art

Stephanie Cowburn

Hubble & Hattie

The Hubble & Hattie imprint was launched in 2009, and is named in memory of two very special Westie sisters owned by Veloce's proprietors. Since the first book, many more have been added, all with the same underlying objective: to be of real benefit to the species they cover; at the same time promoting compassion, understanding and respect between all animals (including human ones!) All Hubble & Hattie publications offer ethical, high quality content and presentation, plus great value for money.

More great books from Hubble & Hattie –

Among the Wolves: Memoirs of a wolf handler (Shelbourne)
Animal Grief: How animals mourn (Alderton)
Babies, kids and dogs – creating a safe & harmonious relationship (Fallon & Davenport)
Because this is our home ... the story of a cat's progress (Bowes)
Bonds – Capturing the special relationship that dogs share with their people (Cukuraite & Pais)
Camper vans, ex-pats & Spanish Hounds: from road trip to rescue – the strays of Spain (Coates & Morris)
Canine Aggression – Rehabilitating an aggressive dog with kindness & compassion (McLennan)
Cat Speak: recognising & understanding behaviour (Rauth-Widmann)
Charlie – The dog who came in from the wild (Tenzin-Dolma)
Clever dog! Life lessons from the world's most successful animal (O'Meara)
Complete Dog Massage Manual, The – Gentle Dog Care (Robertson)
Confessions of a veterinary nurse – Paws, claws and puppy dog tails (Ison)
Detector Dog – A Talking Dogs Scentwork Manual (Mackinnon)
Dieting with my dog: one busy life, two full figures ... and unconditional love (Frezon)
Dinner with Rover: delicious, nutritious meals for you & your dog to share (Paton-Ayre)
Dog Cookies: healthy, allergen-free treat recipes for your dog (Schöps)
Dog-friendly Gardening: creating a safe haven for you & your dog (Bush)
Dog Games – stimulating play to entertain your dog & you (Blenski)
Dog Relax – relaxed dogs, relaxed owners (Pilguj)
Dog Speak: recognising & understanding behaviour (Blenski)
Dogs just wanna have Fun! (Murphy)
Dogs on Wheels: travelling with your canine companion (Mort)
Emergency First Aid for dogs: at home & away Revised Edition (Bucksch)
Exercising your puppy: a gentle & natural approach – Gentle Dog Care (Robertson & Pope)
For the love of Scout: promises to a small dog (Ison)
Fun and Games for Cats (Seidl)
Gods, ghosts, and black dogs – the fascinating folklore & mythology of dogs (Coren)
Harry & his Grownups – A guide to training Parents (Dicks)
Heart-felt dogs – The canines behind the art (Cowburn)
Helping minds meet – skills for a better life with your dog (Zulch & Mills)
Home alone – and happy! Essential life skills for preventing separation anxiety in dogs and puppies (Mallatratt)
Hounds who heal: It's a kind of magic (Kent)
Know Your Dog – The guide to a beautiful relationship (Birmelin)
Life skills for puppies – laying the foundation for a loving, lasting relationship (Zuch & Mills)
Lily: one in a million ... A miracle of survival (Hamilton)
Living with an Older Dog – Gentle Dog Care (Alderton & Hall)

Miaow! Cats really are nicer than people! (Moore)
Mike&Scrabble – A guide to training your new Human (Dicks & Scrabble)
Mike&Scrabble Too – Further tips on training your Human (Dicks & Scrabble)
Mike&Scrabble 2018 calendar (Dicks & Scrabble)
My cat has arthritis – but lives life to the full! (Carrick)
My dog has arthritis – but lives life to the full! (Carrick)
My dog has cruciate ligament injury – but lives life to the full! (Haüsler & Friedrich)
My dog has epilepsy – but lives life to the full! (Carrick)
My dog has hip dysplasia – but lives life to the full! (Haüsler & Friedrich)
My dog is blind – but lives life to the full! (Horsky)
My dog is deaf – but lives life to the full! (Willms)
My dog, my Friend: heart-warming tales of canine companionship from celebrities & other extraordinary people (Gordon)
No walks? No worries! Maintaining wellbeing in dogs on restricted exercise (Ryan & Zulch)
Ollie and Nina and ... Daft doggy doings! (Sullivan)
Partners – Everyday working dogs being heroes every day (Walton)
Puppy called Wolfie – A passion for free will teaching (Gregory)
Smellorama – nose games for dogs (Theby)
Swim to recovery: canine hydrotherapy healing – Gentle Dog Care (Wong)
Tale of two horses – A passion for free-will teaching (Gregory)
Tara – the terrier who sailed around the world (Forrester)
The Little House that didn't have a home (Sullivan)
The lucky, lucky leaf – A Horace and Nim Story (Bourgonje & Hoskins)
The supposedly enlightened person's guide to raising a dog (Young & Tenzin-Dolma)
The Truth about Wolves and Dogs: dispelling the myths of dog training (Shelbourne)
Unleashing the healing power of animals: True stories about therapy animals – and what they do for us (Preece-Kelly)
Waggy Tails & Wheelchairs (Epp)
Walking the dog: motorway walks for drivers & dogs revised edition (Rees)
When man meets dog – what a difference a dog makes (Blazina)
Winston ... the dog who changed my life (Klute)
Worzel goes for a walk. Will you come, too? (Pickles & Bourgonje)
Worzel says hello! Will you be my friend? (Pickles & Bourgonje)
Worzel Wooface: The quite very actual adventures of (Pickles)
Worzel Wooface: The quite very actual Terribibble Twos (Pickles)
Worzel Wooface!: Three quite very actual cheers for (Pickles)
You and Your Border Terrier – The Essential Guide (Alderton)
You and Your Cockapoo – The Essential Guide (Alderton)
Your dog and you – understanding the canine psyche (Garratt)

www.hubbleandhattie.com

First published July 2018 by Veloce Publishing Limited, Veloce House, Parkway Farm Business Park, Middle Farm Way, Poundbury, Dorchester, Dorset, DT1 3AR, England. Tel 01305 260068/Fax 01305 250479/email info@hubbleandhattie.com/web www.hubbleandhattie.com ISBN: 978-1-787112-05-6 UPC: 6-36847-01205-2 © Stephanie Cowburn & Veloce Publishing Ltd 2018. All rights reserved. With the exception of quoting brief passages for the purpose of review, no part of this publication may be recorded, reproduced or transmitted by any means, including photocopying, without the written permission of Veloce Publishing Ltd. Throughout this book logos, model names and designations, etc, have been used for the purposes of identification, illustration and decoration. Such names are the property of the trademark holder as this is not an official publication.

Readers with ideas for books about animals, or animal-related topics, are invited to write to the publisher of Veloce Publishing at the above address. British Library Cataloguing in Publication Data – A catalogue record for this book is available from the British Library. Typesetting, design and page make-up all by Veloce Publishing Ltd on Apple Mac. Printed in India by Replika Press.

Heart-felt dogs

The canines behind the art

Introduction

When I was a child I desperately wanted a pet to cuddle and love, and whisper secrets to, but my brothers were allergic to animal hair, which brought on asthma attacks, so I was never allowed this pleasure (although I would have willingly swapped an asthmatic brother for a dog then!). In the interests of family relations, therefore, I waited until I was an adult before welcoming Heidi, a Border Terrier, into our family.

When Hubble and Hattie publisher Jude Brooks approached me to ask whether I would write a book based around those dogs I've made models of, I was delighted. My husband, Christian, and children, James and Lydia, were all really supportive, too, and with so many people already sharing many elements of their dog's character as part of the process of making a replica model, I felt I had got to know their beloved companions very well. Each animal has his or her own life story, and I felt like they were my friends, too.

I could not have written this book without the dogs' wonderful caretakers providing me with insight and information about their best friend; they are due my huge gratitude and thanks for the time and effort spent letting me have photographs of and tales about their dogs to base this book around. I hope that I have remained true to the detail provided.

Sadly, some of the dogs have been created in loving memory of a time that passed too quickly, in which case, I have, I hope, sensitively matched the character and attitude of the animal as described by their carer, and what I believe the dog might say.

As you read this book you will notice that a high percentage of the dogs featured are from rescue centres around the world. Without the fantastic work that these organisations do, the wonderfully loving animals in their care may well have been put to sleep, and denied the pleasure of long walks, loving cuddles, and a home of their own. Thank you to all who support their efforts: even the smallest donation makes a difference.

Stephanie Cowburn
Cheshire

Foreword

Ten years ago, I was walking my dogs in an idyllic country park. Admiring my surroundings, I was distracted by another stunning sight: a flame-haired beauty approaching from the opposite direction. Her lovely locks blended with the autumnal scene, a breathtaking myriad of wonder in one location.

As she noticed my companions and I, her eyes widened and twinkled. She picked up the pace until her initial casual saunter became a steady jog, then a run, then a full sprint. Such energy. Such tenacity. This was Heidi, a beautiful, cheeky Border Terrier.

But enough about Heidi ...

Another radiant redhead walked alongside Heidi: this was Stephanie, who cared for Heidi.

Over the years, I have admired Stephanie's incredible artistry and talent for so accurately capturing her creation's character and life essence. This collection of images of her amazing models is testament to Stephanie's imagination and skill.

Adorable, charismatic, enchanting ...

But, again, enough about Heidi!

Amy Elliot-Smith
Winner of The Beryl Bainbridge Prize for First Time Author, The People's Book Prize, 2013, with *A Guide to Becoming Distinctly Average*. Owner of The Paw Pad, offering doggy daycare and grooming.

Foreword

I remember it well. My doorbell rang, and I immediately snapped out of my hunched-over-desk mode and tried to remember if I was expecting a visitor ... I wasn't, was I?

This thought was soon replaced by the fear that – owing to my initial alarm – I was not 'world-ready.' This was supposed to be a work day, after all, free from human interaction (especially face-to-face), yet here I was, opening the door to see who had stirred me from the safety of my own boring company ...

It was a postman.

I looked down to see he was holding a box addressed to me. Me? Floods of excitement ... What could it be? Who had sent it? What was it for? I squiggled a squiggle to acknowledge receipt, and returned to my cave to study my new favourite thing. A gentle shake: not much movement. Hmmm. A weight check: light. Hmmm, hmmm. A sniff: not a whiff of chocolate. Intriguing.

All that was left to do was open the mysterious parcel. And that's when my ticker skipped a beat, as I knew in an instant what it was, and I knew, too, who had made it – this

was the work of the brilliantly talented Stephanie Cowburn. We'd never met, but I knew of her through the world of Twitter, and I had long been a fan of her felt model creations, which have an unmistakable quality and look of distinction.

I beamed. Before me was a Mudwaffler. *The* Mudwaffler. A character I had created to host an online children's picture book review blog; partly dog, but mostly bear, and here I was holding it in my hands. It was a sight to behold!

I later discovered that the model had been commissioned by none other than Colin West, a true hero of mine, and poetic genius and grandfather of the group – the Pencil Wobblers – of illustrator and writer folk I belong to.

I have received some stonkingly good gifts over the years – there was the longed-for Micro Machines play set I unwrapped when Father Christmas visited in the late eighties (bearing a striking resemblance to my Grandad); then there was the Christmas when my parents surprised my brother and me with a Sega Mega Drive; the Oasis cassette tape that had me under music's spell – and now, the Mudwaffler.

Immediately, my day was lifted: curtains were parted to let in the light, and I felt a spring in my step. It's a strange feeling to be suddenly full of joy – my

Introduction *And* Forewords

The Mudwaffler.

words can't do it justice, but I know that feeling was brought about by the hours of crafting and studying and skill that Stephanie Cowburn had invested in making my Mudwaffler model. What followed was a weekend of the great outdoors with my children, exploring the woods near our home. We searched for the Mudwaffler's nest amongst the trees, and for the little door he most likely uses to enter said tree. We had a great time posing the Mudwaffler and photographing it all – all memories for me to keep. All seeded by Stephanie Cowburn's felting skills.

Without doubt, my experience has been repeated over and over, up and down the country and, indeed, around the globe, whenever a parcel sent by Stephanie Cowburn arrives on a doorstep.

Her felt model creations are not only charming, they are also highly accurate, and capture all the little character details that are often overlooked in a drawing. One of my favourite galleries on her website (stephaniecowburn.com) features a selection of the models she has made next to their real-life counterparts – if this doesn't make you smile, I don't know what will! The likeness is remarkable; I urge you to see for yourself. You'll not be disappointed ... and might even end up with your own doorstep parcel ...

As I write this the Mudwaffler is sitting beside me, delivering that joyous feeling to me all over again. Suddenly, I feel an urge to get outside and climb trees with my children, revelling in our next adventure.

Isn't it amazing?

Karl Newson

Illustrator of *Rupert the Dinosaur* and *Super Chimp*, and writer of *A bear is a bear (except when he's not)*, *Here Comes the Sun*, *Little Grey's Birthday Surprise,* and *Fum*.

Meg

Border Collie Commissioned by Lyn Hall

"Why are people so untidy? Why do they wander off in different directions when you've just neatly herded them together? Why do people need to have a 'sit down' after walking only eight miles? What are shoelaces for other than to be chewed and pulled undone?

Why do humans get cross when you bark a warning about unexpected intruders? Why do they object to me helping myself to snacks in the kitchen when they're helping themselves all the time? Why do they think I'm being naughty when I'm just taking the initiative to have a bit of fun?

I don't think I shall ever know the answers of all these questions, or understand people, either! I can't help but love them, though, and want to defend and protect them ... I just wish they'd stay still long enough for me to do it!"

Meg

"I didn't eat ALL of it: I saved you the crumbs ..."

Posy

Alsatian/Rhodesian Ridgeback cross
Commissioned by Siobhan McClelland

" As a young pup, my life began on the doorstep of the RSPCA shelter after I was abandoned, which has always made me a little bit anxious about everything. Luckily for me, I found a loving home where I was very much wanted, and settled in quickly.

I couldn't ever claim that I do everything I *should* do – I had a bad start in life, so need to look out for myself – but I'll gladly show off my fab playbow, and give my paw if there's a reasonable chance of a generous titbit or two.

One of my hobbies is chasing birds: I love the noise they make when I surprise them and they fly away, especially if there are a few of them together. I wonder if I make them feel anxious ...? "

Posy

"They've gone out again – I wonder when they'll be back ...?"

Heidi

Border Terrier   Commissioned by Christian Cowburn

"My ideal job would be a 'professional biscuit tester,' but I'd be happy to extend the role to cover just 'food,' and even 'non food' stuff! I'll eat almost anything – or at least give it a try. After 'food tester' my next job choice would be 'professional toy tester.' To date, my record for destroying a toy is within two minutes: de-squeaking it in under 30 seconds, and leaving the stuffing strewn across the floor for the servants to clear up. I am a legend! For relaxation I like to cuddle up with my Mum on the sofa, though she does have a habit of sneaking off when my eyes are closed; sometimes even to the kitchen where tasty things are kept on high shelves and in the fridge. To try and prevent this from happening, I either lay on top of her or keep one paw touching her at all times so that she can't get away without me noticing ... and I can follow her like a furry shadow to monitor her snack intake, and remind her that mine is low!"

Heidi

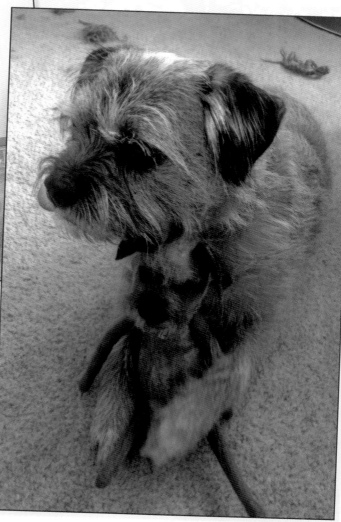

*"I helped myself ...
was that okay?"*

Willow

Miniature Schnauzer/German Shepherd cross

Commissioned by Paula Reynolds

"I went to live with Mum and Dad on their first wedding anniversary, which means I'm very special, just like my kennel name of 'Arbey Something Special.'

Hat stands, Welsh dressers, and other pieces of furniture have all benefited from having nibbled edges that make them 'Willow Special.' I like having things in my mouth – preferably food, despite a lot of it upsetting my tummy. My favourite toy that I love to carry around is my duck, which always has a soggy beak from where I suck it.

I hate finding leaves or twigs attached to my fur, and, when this happens, I refuse to walk a step further until the offending cling-on is removed.

I am 'something special' after all!"

Willow

*"Have you seen my duck,
by any chance ...?"*

Princess

Pit Bull Terrier   Commissioned by Chris Khoa

"Despite my muscular, tough exterior I'm a real softy, really, and don't have a mean bone in my body. I just love everyone and they love me, too!

At the park I introduce myself to the other dogs and their people, and always go back to my Dad when he wants me to, even if he just signals with his hand that it's time to go. I'm what people call 'well trained,' but I call it 'eager to please.'

I love my family, and will do anything for them. Even if I'm starving after a long day swimming in the sea, I'll let my brothers eat first, even though I'm strong enough to easily push in. I'm sensitive like that; so sensitive that I suffer from allergies, especially on my ears: lucky for me that my Dad puts some good medicine on them when they get itchy and sore."

Princess

"Posture is very important: chin in, chest out, shoulders back!"

Morphie

Jack Russell

Commissioned by Tracy Brady

" Some say that becoming a professional football player is a sign of a misspent youth – and maybe it is – though you still need to have talent to be picked for the team. I would have liked to have played for Liverpool football club, or the England team, of course, but somehow my running and dribbling the ball talents were overlooked.

I did hear an outrageous rumour that I'm not much of a team player: keeping the ball to myself, and not passing often enough. But when you're the best player on the field – and the only one who can head a ball correctly – surely it's your responsibility to keep hold of it?

Whatever. Their loss. I still enjoy playing in an amateur capacity, even if it hasn't brought me fame and fortune ... and a string of adoring fans! "

Morphie

"I'm ready for
action – get your
shoes on; let's go!"

Jackie

Greyhound

Commissioned by Elizabeth Hill

"I have a history of racing, which I really hated, so I plotted to get out of the industry by coming last in all my races. My plan worked like a dream, and I was sent to a rescue centre before being rehomed.

My Mum says I'm part-monkey and part-cat because I climb up on top of things to sit down. I can't see the point of standing up longer than is completely necessary, and the more reclined I am, the better!

When I'm at the park I make sure everyone knows that although I'm only small, I'm the one in charge, and that excessive revelry in my company is frowned upon. If I'm not behaving in an excitable manner, then no one should overstep the mark."

Jackie

"So, anyway,
that's the story of
my life ... Hey!
You haven't
fallen asleep ...
have you?"

Mckinsey

Border Collie/German Shepherd cross

Commissioned by Martha Ruman

"I really like water, puddles, streams and rivers; the wetter the better! A while ago my Mum became poorly for a really long time, and ended up being housebound, which meant that I spent most of my time at home keeping her company and looking after her. As a reward for being her special carer, I got to go on car journeys to the river which I adore, and I also love the car – so much that when Dad came home from work I would insist we do a couple of circuits of the drive with me.

After my Mum got better, as a surprise they took me to Florida, not to see Mickey Mouse but the ocean – the big, wide-open ocean full of water and waves and hours of fun, splashing and diving.

I absolutely loved it! Who needs Mickey Mouse when you can have the sea?"

22

McKinsey

"Are we going out? Soon, maybe?"

Dougie

Wire-haired Dachshund

Commissioned by Barry Weldon

I am Mr Independent, and not at all what you'd call a 'cuddly' guy.

No, sir: I like my own space and I like my own way too!

When my dinner is being prepared, I like to run around the garden working up an appetite, letting all the pigeons know it's my dinnertime. The 'dinner lady' and the neighbours don't find this quite as entertaining as we do, and shout for me to be quiet, the spoil sports!

Sometimes I like to surprise my people by snuggling up to them (not something I do very often) but, just as they're thinking 'Oh, how lovely! Dougie's being all snuggly' out comes my tongue straight into their cup of tea.

Oh yeah, fooled 'em again!

Dougie

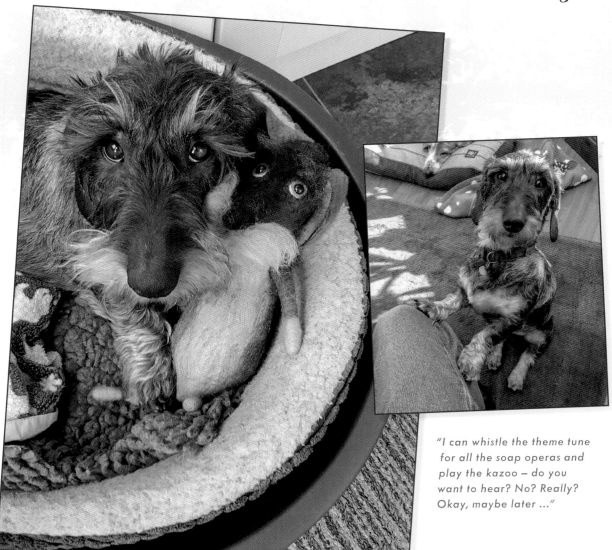

"I can whistle the theme tune for all the soap operas and play the kazoo — do you want to hear? No? Really? Okay, maybe later ..."

Diesel

Staffordshire Bull Terrier

Commissioned by Tytti Luukkainen

" That famous chap Ricky Gervais is a patron of a rescue charity called All Dogs Matter, and he tweeted a picture of me on Twitter where it received thousands of 'likes' and retweets, and I was an internet sensation!

Shortly after this, I was taken home by a family who, sadly, had recently lost their previous rescue dog. They originally wanted a gundog but ended up with a 'fun dog' – me! I'm totally goofy, love to make people laugh, adore chasing lizards in the foothills of the Pyrenees where I live – and where it gets pretty hot. My thoughtful family provides me with a shallow bucket of water to cool off in as I haven't learnt to swim, yet.

I don't see that as a problem, though: it's not as if my life depends on it ... "

Diesel

"You look familiar: have we met before?"

Tilly

Miniature Schnauzer
Commissioned by Emily Warren

"My Mum went on a tour around Europe for seven weeks a couple of years ago, leaving me in Australia with my grandparents (who spoilt me rotten, as all grandparents do). Before Mum set off she had a model of me made, which she collected on her trip to England, and then travelled through Europe with a 'mini me' model in her handbag, which she said was just like having me with her, 'only quieter.'

Meanwhile, at the grandparents' house I was living it up on homemade meals, treats pretty much on-demand, country walks, and a long snooze in the afternoons.

But seven weeks feels like a lifetime when you miss your Mum, and I was so pleased to see her when she got back. I've told her that, in future, a two-week holiday is more than enough!"

Tilly

"This is my innocent look: I haven't really hidden your passport, mum ..."

Fluffy

Norfolk Terrier cross

Commissioned by Fiona Russell-White

"I'm quite particular about how I like things done now that I'm an old lady. I like meals to be homemade, and none of that crunchy ready-meal stuff that's straight out of a packet. I like my steak or chicken cooked to perfection, with a side order of rice or pasta.

My meals are nice tummy-fillers, and set me up for chasing away rabbits, birds and hedgehogs who trespass in the garden. Call me old-fashioned but I do love the scent of cowpats, and roll to my heart's content in a fresh one given the opportunity!

I spend my holidays with my aunt and uncle who let me sleep in their bed with them: no cold kennels for me, just pure Egyptian cotton sheets and comfort all the way!"

"Any chance of a snack
before X Factor starts?"

Daisy

Bassett Hound

Commissioned by Annette Mercer

"I've had a long and rewarding life, but I'm old and tired now: you only need look at my droopy eyes to see that. All I really want to do these days is sleep or have my tummy rubbed whilst I reminisce about my youthful ambitions and misdemeanors.

My person thinks it's good for my 'constitution' to take some fresh air and exercise on a daily basis, so she shakes my lead and cries 'walkies' in an excited, high-pitched voice that only dogs can hear.

I can't be bothered to move, however, unless it's to see if there's anything in my food bowl. I like eating, but I definitely need a bigger bowl that will accommodate my ears as well as my food!"

"When I said feel free to go and chat with someone else, what I actually meant was please go away and let me sleep!"

Cherry

Chocolate Labrador

Commissioned by Gavin Berriman

"I really enjoy it when guests come to the house for dinner. They're so friendly and polite that it seems rude not to reciprocate, especially whilst they eat their dinner. So I like to sit directly in front of them, licking my lips in appreciation of the good food they have the pleasure of eating, and – occasionally, but not often enough – food they share with me.

Nobody here seems to think that I'm a particularly bright dog – I've heard them say that I could get lost in my own home – which is cheeky, because I know where the kitchen is and how to find my bed, so life is good. What else does a dog need to know?

I do love going fishing by the river, and I'm happy to sit for hours quietly contemplating what might be for dinner, and whether I can remember the way home ..."

Cherry

"Hello, have we met before? Oh, we have!"

Dot

Whippet   Commissioned by Katie Wall

"Whoever mentioned in passing that I'm not allowed upstairs should have put it in writing, because I'll sneak up there and into the children's beds at every opportunity.

Children smell so clean and nice at bedtime: like they've been washed and prepared specially for my benefit. I'm often unceremoniously removed from their cosy beds, however, and have to find a warm lap to lay on downstairs instead.

For one hour out of every 24 I like to move – run, even – really fast, chasing balls, which I confess I'm totally obsessed with. I show off to the neighbourhood dogs just how fast I can chase the ball. I'm racing after it like lightning; then, just like thunder, I snore for the next 23 hours ...

36

"One day I'll fly away ..."

Molly

Tri-coloured Border Collie

Commissioned by Anne Butler

" When you live in the beautiful Scottish hills, it's only natural to take up hill walking and mountain climbing. My Mum is very active in this respect, and loves an adventure as much as I do. We have stayed in tents (which can be a bit draughty), bed and breakfasts, bothes, and even hotels (really posh ones, too!).

We travel by car, train, boat and kayak to get to our destinations. 'Adventure' is my middle name, but there's also nothing better than a post-adventure, full-body massage from my Mum before playing and chilling out with my friends or chasing my ball.

Life is one long holiday for me, it seems. "

Molly

"A rest? Why do you need a rest: we've only walked 8 miles ...!"

Holly

Labradoodle

Commissioned by Rachel Watts

"Is it nearly teatime? I did eat breakfast this morning, and had a few sneaky biscuits that Mum baked. They're so moreish – you can't beat homemade cookies – but my tummy is telling me that it must be teatime, or at least time for a light snack or two.

I'm so active – walking, bouncing, running and jumping everywhere I go – that I burn off the calories, and have to refuel. I find it hard waiting for mealtimes to come around, and probably get a bit vocal. Mum calls me a 'Diva,' which is not a term I'm familiar with … is it another way of saying 'hungry'?"

Holly

*"I'm worried I might
have missed breakfast
... not today, necessarily,
but maybe sometime
last week?"*

41

Toby

Jack Russell

Commissioned by Tony De Saules

" Me? I'm a professional shade-snoozer, country explorer and mountaineer. Having short legs is no restriction when it comes to mountain climbing, oh no. I took Mt Snowdon and Scafell Pike in my stride amongst other hills and mountains in Great Britain.

My love of the great outdoors extends to camping with my people. They're a bit soft, though, and like camping in a van, which, truth be told, suits me fine as I much prefer a nice sofa and a comfy bed to sleep on. The van is a home-from-home after a long day's walking or climbing, and my wet fur and soggy paws dry much quicker than they do in a tent. There's nothing worse than that embarrassing 'wet dog' smell, is there?! "

Toby

*"I'm not sulking,
I'm deep in
thought!"*

Tacy

Shih Tzu

Commissioned by Joseph Castenando

"I'm named after a character played by Lucille Ball in the Hollywood movie *The long, long trailer*, and, like all Hollywood actresses, I'm a little bit spoilt, indulged, needy, and highly opinionated. My very reliable internal clock gives me the authority to remind my people when they should be switching off the lights, locking up for the night, and taking themselves off to bed. We girls need our beauty sleep, after all.

I have a good grasp on what I like, and will only engage with my people if they're offering me what I want: otherwise I can be deaf to unreasonable requests, remaining aloof until my mood changes or there are treats on offer ..."

44

Tacy

"If you're thinking of nipping out later, can you get me something from the shops?"

Orion

Long-haired Dachshund
Commissioned by Eduardo Klein Fichtner

" I'm from Brazil ... a Brazilian ... a long-haired Brazilian, but I don't *have* a 'Brazilian,' whatever that might be!

What I do have is an obsession with socks. They're like floppy snakes that smell like feet, and are so much fun to rip into little pieces. I do this so that they can't eat my people's feet with their wide, open mouths, and clearly I'm doing a really good job as Dad keeps bringing more into the house for me to tackle.

I like to have control of the household, and if I need a midnight comfort break then everyone will know about it ... then again at 3am and 5am ... What? I'm a small dog with a small bladder and very accommodating parents who really don't mind getting out of their comfy warm bed to open the door for me several times each night ... "

46

Orion

*"I wonder what you can see
from way up there ...?"*

Otka

German Shepherd

Commissioned by Chris Murray

" I used to think that my ideal job would be working as a quality control officer in the pet food industry, tasting the newly-improved recipes to see if they actually *had* improved.

However, the job I currently do – I'm a guide dog for the blind and partially-sighted – requires a lot more qualifications and training, and is ultimately more rewarding.

It's a big responsibility to keep someone safe, making sure that they don't step into the path of a car, or walk into things.

The rewards and perks of the job are excellent – everyone admires my hard work and dedication – though the best bit is that I can sneak extra teatime treats right from under my person's nose! "

"I do like being in the garden, although I'm not really green-fingered: more brown-pawed from digging!"

49

'Puppy' Bella

Spaniel   Commissioned by George O'Wilson-Howell

" Mum was in the pet shop buying food for our rescue dog (my brother), when she saw me, and instantly fell in love with my big brown eyes! My real name is Bella but, as I didn't seem to grow much and always remained small and petite like a puppy, that's what I became known as.

Sadly, even though *I* haven't grown much, my hair has, which means that, every few weeks, I have to go to the groomers. They're actually very nice there, but when I come home all perfumed and clipped, I feel a bit naked, especially when my brothers sniff me all over to make sure it's still me!

Me and my brothers go crazy sometimes, running circuits around the garden like we're competing in the doggy Olympics. Mostly, though, I like sitting in the shade watching them, or next to my Grandma Mae, waiting for my hair to grow back! "

50

'Puppy' Bella

"What do you mean you
need to see my ID? I'm older
than I look, you know!:"

Ned

Whippet   Commissioned by Katie Wall

"Honestly, butter wouldn't melt in my mouth. I am such a gentle, honest and thoughtful gentleman ... except when there are tasty morsels of illicit food on the kitchen worktop, when, maybe, I'm not quite so honest ... or thoughtful ... There was one occasion when a whole bag of marshmallows had been left out for me to help myself to. They're really weird things to eat, though, like sugary pillows of foam – tasty, but really hard to swallow – so I hid them all around the house until I felt ready to tackle another one. Mum was finding half-eaten, fluffy, dog hair-coated marshmallows in varying states of decay for several days afterwards!

I've never been allowed to live it down. In my defense, had it been roast chicken on offer, I'd have left no evidence whatsoever!"

52

Ned

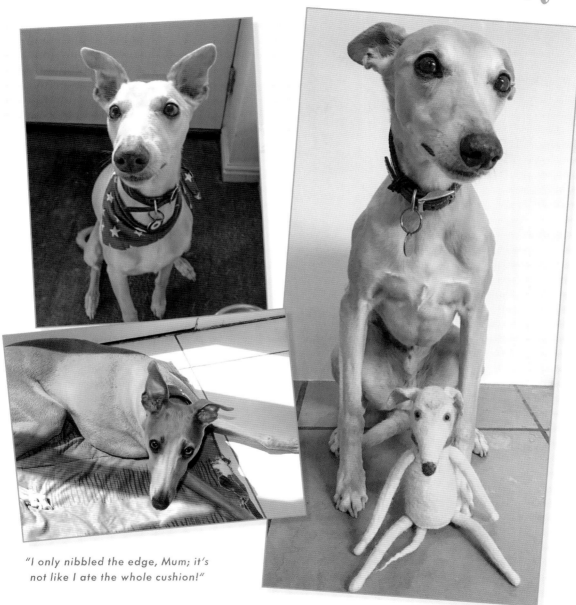

"I only nibbled the edge, Mum; it's
not like I ate the whole cushion!"

'Turbo' Tess

Border Collie
Commissioned by Mary Myatt

"As my name suggests, I'm something of a whirlwind who can keep going for as long as you can throw a ball or a stick for my pleasure and amusement. I'm happy to give you a couple of minutes' rest, now and then, though you will need to build your stamina.

I come from the sheep dog aristocracy in Cheshire in the UK, so therefore deserve the rapt attention of everyone. When 'everyone' isn't looking, however, I bury my toys and balls in the flowerbeds. It's an amusing game that no one else seems to find that funny. It's the perfect way of getting replacement toys, too!"

'Turbò Tess

"Time to play – I'll hide; you seek!"

Jack

Labradoodle   Commissioned by Rachel Watts

" Hi, I'm Jack! Don't mind me – I'm very happy to just sit quietly whilst you work or have a chat. You'll barely know I'm here, but, if you do have a minute to stroke me or tickle behind my ears, I'd quite like you to do that until you get cramp in your hand.

With my big brown eyes and hairy eyebrows, I'm fairly confident you won't mind ... you can always swap hands if one gets too tired.

I quite like outdoor pursuits like cross country running, swimming, and ornithology. I like getting up close to the birds for detailed inspection, but they're strange little things: flying away before I can get close enough to see the whites of their eyes! "

56

Jack

"I can't remember if I turned off the lights and locked the door ... hmmm."

Ennis

Staffy cross Commissioned by Sarah Lowe

"I wear this device called a muzzle when I'm out and about because other dogs sometimes upset me. When I was younger, see, I mixed with the wrong crowd who led me astray: I'm very sorry about that now, but I knew no better.

The foster family who took me in didn't really want a Staffy cross, and especially not a cross Staffy like me, but I'm happy to say that we all fell in love with each other, and they gave me a forever home.

When we go to the beach (which I love), I dig really big holes and roll on the sand. The best bit, though, is when we stop off for ice cream – that's just heaven!

I totally adore my family: they're all cuddle-monsters and really kissy people. When we cuddle, for a laugh, I sometimes pinch my mum's hair bobble from her ponytail ... she doesn't always laugh, though ..."

58

Ennis

*"I love digging so much
I'm thinking of becoming
an archaeologist."*

Cricket Lipkin

Pomapoo   Commissioned by Barrett Lipkin

" It always sounds so weird when people call me a 'dog,' as I always think of myself as more human than canine, especially with my extensive vocal range. I see Mum and Dad as my equals because we do absolutely everything together! When they're eating I make sure I'm eating; when they're playing with their phones I'm playing with my toy pony; when they're playing ball, I'm playing ball, too.

The pair of them are ball-mad, you know: they love to throw it and kick it; it's very sweet watching them play, although they haven't quite mastered the art of fetching the ball, yet, so I like to set a good example and do that for them.

When my legs grow a bit more I'm planning to learn how to drive the car because I love travelling, and Mum and Dad take me out wherever they go. I'm totally fearless, so visiting new places and experiencing new things doesn't worry them ... especially if they've got me with them! "

Cricket Lipkin

"And here we are, settling down for our after-lunch siesta ... I love looking back through my holiday snaps ..."

Sammy

Labrador Commissioned by Julie Tutssel

"I've been described as 'very musical,' as I sing along when my young person practices his saxophone. It doesn't seem to matter that I don't know all the words, because he doesn't seem to get the notes right all the time, either.

I think I'm from a musical family because I remember, when I was a puppy, making my people howl after I'd chewed through the kitchen table and chairs whilst they were out ... I like a challenge, too – shoes, address books, homework, and electrical cables (they give me a buzz) – but I've upped my game recently by chewing the plaster off the wall: that and the kitchen table got me some serious attention and respect.

Like all Labradors I adore my food, and will outstare anybody when they're eating. They call me 'Sammy the Stalker' because my eyes follow the food as it travels plate-to-mouth, plate-to-mouth ... and occasionally plate-to-floor!"

Sammy

"What can I chew
next, I wonder ...?"

Boue

Spaniel A gift to Jo Douthwaite

"My people are multilingual, and thought that it would be funny to call me Boue (which is French for 'mud) because, apparently, I'm the colour of mud.

I think, however, that I have the last laugh because, as it turns out, I do really love a nice, muddy puddle, and adore swimming in murky rivers. When I walk muddy pawprints around the house, I keep hearing "Oh, Boue!"

Roughly translated this means 'Oh, mud!' Which is exactly what it is!"

Boue

"I can't do a thing with my hair once it gets wet!"

Eddy

Abour Cojack cross Commissioned by Carina Mack

"I was discovered wandering the streets when I was about three years old – lost, abandoned, forgotten – I don't know which it was, but the family who took me home are so lovely and kind that, at first, it made me anxious every time they went out and left me alone, as I never knew whether they were coming back to feed me.

I had to improvise when this happened, and would help myself to scones, and empty the bread bin so that I had something to eat. When they came home, to my surprise my people were not pleased that I'd managed to get my own dinner: I'd eaten theirs, it seemed, and they didn't fancy mine!"

"Me and my shadow!"

Immie

Cyprus Poodle   Commissioned by Jude Brooks

"Coming from Northern Cyprus, I'm what you might call a 'chilled-out pooch' with a sunny disposition and lots of love to give. I like to keep up with the trends, and attending yoga classes with my mum is a great way of increasing our core strength and suppleness. My favourite yoga positions are downward facing dog and extended puppy pose.

Mum and I are best friends, and go everywhere together (I like the pub the best). Between you and me, I have to keep a close eye on her at work, checking her spelling and writing – a bit like a sub editor or personal assistant.

I love being in the office, listening to the chatter and banter. I always feel like I've done a good day's work come home-time!"

Immie

"Yoga? Don't you mean Doga?!"

Maverick

German Wire-haired Pointer   Commissioned by David Snazdell

> Every year we go on holiday to Loughrigg, in the UK, where we do my special walk. 'Maverick's walk,' goes up and over some rocks that Mum and Dad take pictures of me standing on every time we're there. Year-by-year those rocks seem to have got smaller and I have got bigger!
>
> I love it there, chasing Dad as he races downhill at full speed on his bike, Mum shouting after us "Slow down, he doesn't like it!" But I love it, really, so always smile and wink at Dad ... and we go even faster!
>
> I love running more than anything, but next on my list would be sitting in a window, contentedly watching the world go by. I'm not fussy which window, either; it can be one at home or in a café. I shout greetings to people passing the house but if I'm in the café I don't bother.
>
> It's nice, sometimes, to have a quiet afternoon without meeting anyone you know.

Maverick

*"I wonder where
we'll go on our
next holiday ... the
Caribbean, maybe?"*

Hase

German Shepherd Commissioned by Stephanie Aldag

"I began life as a neglected puppy in Lebanon, from where I was flown to France by a rescue organization, and offered for adoption (on more than one occasion).

Apparently, I was too 'difficult,' but I wasn't, really: I was just scared, so would do the wrong thing and get smacked for it.

Eventually, I was adopted by a family who had other German Shepherds, and felt right at home: my new pals helped me to settle in and trust people.

They gave me the French name of Angst-Hase, which means 'Afraid Bunny.' I'm not at all afraid, now, and love people and other dogs. Long walks and warm hugs are what I love most of all."

Hase

"Why won't you speak? Don't you love me any more?"

Chico

Chihuahua   Commissioned by Jake Shaw

"I should have been an actor, daaahling; clearly, I was made for the stage, bright lights, fame, and adoring hoards of fans clamoring for my attention. I'd have loved it all, every minute of it, and so would my sidekick Mr Rabbit (he's just a puppet but we're good friends, and I love him with all my heart).

I'm sure that if Hollywood had seen me the casting directors would have found me a starring role, or written parts especially for me. Wherever I go I'm admired and loved by strangers and friends alike. If they forget to pay me full attention momentarily, I remind them of my presence with a whimper or a little nudge.

Chico Shaw, the greatest Chihuahua who ever lived!"

74

Chico

"Bring on the bright lights and adoring fans!"

Mae

Kaninchen Dachshund   Commissioned by Fiona Eldridge

" I may well be small, but I have a really big heart, and just love to be picked up and cuddled by everyone I meet. It also saves my little legs from getting tired.

When I moved from Spain to England, I brought that lovely Spanish siesta tradition with me – there's nothing nicer than a good nap in the afternoon after a busy morning socializing.

Despite my little legs, I make sure that all the bigger dogs know who's boss. If their people are about I play a trick on the dogs, screaming and crying loudly, which makes the people think that their pooches are hurting me, and I get all the fuss.

Like I said, I'm the boss – it works every time! "

Mae

"I'm so tired from just walking to the front door ... what? Your legs are much longer than mine!"

Poppy

Parsons Jack Russell/Collie cross

Commissioned by Kate Taylor

"Beyond a good fish supper washed down with a wholesome glass of milk, my favourite things in life are balls. I love 'em: tennis balls, footballs, squeaky balls and ping pong balls – the more the merrier! I love how they roll on the ground and bounce and spin through the air. I love to chase them and chew them ... ahhh how I adore balls!

In-between playing with balls, I like to keep my family company, and hate the idea that they might encounter a 'ball' situation without me. They might not know what to do, so I go everywhere with them ... you know, just in case."

Poppy

"Being a ball girl at Wimbledon is my lifelong ambition."

Banjo

Whippet

Commissioned by Tina Watmough

" My Mum thinks I have a split personality, though it's more a case of mild bipolar. One minute I'm running like the wind, playing with my friends at the park or in the woods, the life and soul of the party ... and then the next all I want to do is curl up under my duvet and sleep for hours at a time.

The only thing that gets me out from under the duvet is the smell of illicit food – pizza, pasta, roast dinners, crisps ... you name it, I can sniff it out from the depths of a 4-tog duvet! "

80

Banjo

"Well, hello girls!"

Macy

Jack Russell   Commissioned by Simon Taylor

"I was born without a back paw, would you believe, and for 18 months kept getting grazes and infections in my stump ... so Mum and Dad decided to ask the vet to cut off my entire leg! Can you imagine that? Waking up without your leg?

Honestly, I can't tell you what a relief it was: I suddenly found that I could balance better, and run – oh, how I could run! My friends at the park who all have the full complement of legs are hard-pushed to keep up with me, and I get so close to the squirrels that I can see the whites of their eyes!

Disabled? Me? No way, Jose: I'm Racy Macy!"

"Catch me if
you can!"

Jovie

Maltese cross Commissioned by Brian Marable

" I was born in Spain, where I was left in a field with my two brothers, to be found by a lovely lady who bottle-fed us day and night until we were big enough to go to a rescue centre, where another lovely lady from France gave us a home and took great care of us.

One day, this lady decided to sell a chair – even though there was nothing wrong with it! – and another really lovely lady came to buy it. She fell in love with me at the same time, and, eventually, the chair and I went to live with this new lovely lady who introduced me to her family; my new family.

Soon afterwards we all moved to America, where there are loads of squirrels, who are just the most fun to chase. I love playing with the kids, my sisters: we jump on the trampoline together and play ball endlessly. I love to sneak into Mom and Dad's bed for cuddles when there isn't a kid taking up the space in-between them, and I have mastered the art of pouting if I don't get my own way (which I usually do!). "

Jovie

"A dog isn't just for Christmas ..."

Heinz

German Shepherd

Commissioned by Stephanie Aldag

"G'day, mate. Do you mind if I give you the once over? As head of security in New South Wales, Australia, I love being intimidating and scary. I find it works well as visitors are pretty wary of calling, so my job of protecting my Mum and the family is a cinch. Little do these people know, however, I'm a big-hearted softy ... but don't tell anyone as my reputation will be shot!

Once, we adopted a fledgling Magpie called Trulla. We were the best of buddies and, just for laughs, Trulla and I would spook the neighbour's dogs. I'd bark really loudly whilst Trulla ambushed them from overhead – ha ha – how we laughed!

Eventually, Trulla found her wings and flew away, so to speak ... no worries ... I know she's having fun, I miss her but I'm laidback about it, and the Aussie sun always puts me in a good mood.

Good on ya, Trulla!"

Heinz

"Stop telling everyone I'm a big softy, it does nothing for my street cred!"

Louis

Bichon Frise   Commissioned by Katy-Ann Webb

"Now that I'm getting on a bit I prefer a gentler, home-based routine. I no longer enjoy going for walks as my hips are stiff and, with being shortsighted and hard of hearing, everything takes me by surprise. It's embarrassing to literally bump into people you know but not recognize them.

It's easier to stay at home. I like to be waited on and, if my water isn't fresh enough, I complain to the 'staff' (also fondly known as the 'family'), who provide me with fresh water and treats on demand.

I refuse to eat 'dog food,' preferring freshly-cooked chicken, shredded and beautifully presented. I'm named after an old French king, so expect to be treated like one!"

Louis

"It's not much fun
getting old – try
and avoid it!"

Gretel

Bernese Mountain dog

Commissioned by Mandy Farrow

"
Life is short so my motto is 'take it seriously and make the most of it.' This doesn't include acting the fool, wasting time, or 'having a laugh,' and I'm happy to give out disapproving looks whilst on patrol. I did not earn the title of 'fun police' by messing about ...

When I'm off duty (which isn't very often, as I'm dedicated to stamping out those frivolous folk having too much fun), I'm family-orientated, and protect them by seeing off delivery men with my deep, throaty bark.

Who knows what they might be trying to deliver ... party packs or joke books ... I don't think so!
"

Gretel

"Can you turn down that music?
You're keeping me awake!"

Jupp

German Shepherd
Commissioned by Tatjana Hoenich

"I come from a long line of police dogs. I've got fifteen brothers and sisters who are all trained officers, sniffing out and solving crimes. I'm very proud of this. Even my Dad works for the police force ... not as a sniffer dog, obviously – he's paid with that money stuff, not biscuits.

Despite my family connection with the force, I'm a stay-at-home domestic dog with big ideas of guarding the family and keeping them safe. I have to be kept away from family friends because I find it hard to distinguish the difference between friend and foe until I have my teeth firmly implanted in their leg ... only kidding – I'm never actually given the chance to get that close!"

Jupp

"Can you see me?"

Zuki

Cavapoo   Commissioned by Hazel Winstanley

"I'm what my Mum lovingly calls a 'Diva.' We travel all around Great Britain together, trying out dog-friendly places to play in, eat in, and stay. I'm often photographed with a delicious plate of food in front of me, which I refuse to eat until it has been chopped into tiny Zuki-mouth-sized pieces. A girl has her standards, you know!

When we stay overnight somewhere, I get to sleep on the comfy beds after sampling the meals that the hotel has on offer.

Naturally, I insist we only travel first class. Nothing else is good enough for Diva Zuki!"

Zuki

"Yes, darling,
first class all
the way!"

Chico

Spaniel   Commissioned by Lucy Grishholm

"When I bark I have that soft, southern Irish lilt to my voice that everyone finds so endearing – that and my good looks and exciting Irish lifestyle! I help my Dad, going everywhere he does like a furry, brown-and-white shadow. He runs (or I should say, we run) boat trips, which are very popular, as well as coaching coastal rowing teams.

We're kept very busy with our jobs but we don't let stress get to us, oh no: we make sure we find time to relax and go the pub before falling asleep in the chair.

It's the sea breeze, a clear conscience, and hard work that helps us sleep so soundly."

Chico

"Come on, let's go to the pub!"

Hamish

Longhaired Dachshund   Commissioned by Penny Delaney

"Mum tells the story of how I was rescued from a breeder who didn't treat me very well. Apparently, I would squash myself into the corner of my crate and whimper when anyone came to open the door. All I remember now is the gentle look of love on her face, and how kind she was to me. She's bought me lots of toys, though I haven't got a clue what I'm meant to do with them.

The life I had before caused me to need extensive dental work, and I ended up with only six teeth! You can't do much damage with six teeth – not even to your food!

I used to be scared of feet which, when you have short legs, are quite close to your head at all times. I realized feet weren't anything to be scared of when the young boy person hid popcorn between his toes, probably to eat later, but I'd sneak up and eat it before he could put his socks back on."

Hamish

"I want a quiet uncomplicated life: that's not much to ask for ... is it?"

Lou

German Shepherd   Commissioned by Rose Anne O'Reilly Shrum

"My little sister was a Chihuahua called Juicy. She was tiny and bossy, and my absolute best friend in the whole world, but she got poorly and died, and I miss her terribly.

Juicy didn't like getting her feet wet, but would happily watch me jump the tidal waves and race around the beach at top speed. I love the beach: the sand between my toes, the breeze in my fur, and the water up my nose! It's all wonderful and I especially love the water.

When I got home, all beach-sleepy and cuddly, Juicy and I would curl up together and snooze until it was dinner time. I miss that.

I love the snow in winter, too. Juicy used to wear her sweaters and complain about her cold feet but I love rolling and bounding through it. It is just frozen water, after all, and I love water!"

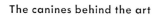

"Race you into the sea!"

Sprocket

Springer Spaniel   Commissioned by Daniel Pidge

"I'm not your typical bouncy energetic Spaniel because I like a quiet life – which some might mistake for laziness. I don't see anything wrong in sleeping all day – energy conservation is high on my agenda because I like to reserve it for when my Dad gets home from work.

Dad is my best pal, and we go to the beach to crab in rock pools and paddle at low tide. I remind Dad that throwing a ball is good for him by repeatedly giving him one to throw. This does mean that I have to run after it, of course, but I see it as part of my duty to keep him active and fit.

I'm fascinated by bins – bedroom bins, kitchen bins, any type, really. It's surprising what people throw away these days: tissues, ear buds, tasty wrappers with the smell left on, what a waste!"

102

Sprocket

*"Oh, no, it wasn't me ... were they
really your favourite slippers ...?"*

Rasmus

Pointer   Commissioned by Tytti Luukkainen

"I was abandoned when I was a tiny puppy, but, luckily, found on the streets in Italy by a kind lady who I insisted should take me home.

She is wonderful, and has given me everything a dog could want — food, toys, love, warmth, and a safe forever home. She even got me my own passport so that I can travel and see the world, although I never travel alone — I always take the family with me, it's only polite!"

Rasmus

"Now then ... where shall we go next on our travels?"

Fluffy Elizabeth Star

Bichon Frise   Commissioned by Natalie Elward

" It's been said that I am old before my time, but I see this as intuitive wisdom. I have the ability to see people for what they are: tummy-ticklers, housemaids and personal chefs, in essence.

I adore human food, there's such an abundance of it, and also love other animals. I'm really not that fussed about people, though, and I'm not shy about letting them know it! In general, I'd rather hide under the table, curled in a tight ball, until they go away.

I've been married (just the once) to Twinkle for eight years, and between us we raised five gorgeous puppies who mysteriously disappeared, one by one ... we never did find out where they went. "

106

Fluffy Elizabeth Star

"Don't you think I'm just the cutest girl you've ever seen?"

Farley

Terrier cross

Commissioned by Barbara Zebrowski

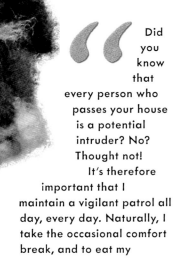

"Did you know that every person who passes your house is a potential intruder? No? Thought not!

It's therefore important that I maintain a vigilant patrol all day, every day. Naturally, I take the occasional comfort break, and to eat my meals, but the safety of my family is paramount, regardless of my modest size.

Over the years I have disciplined myself to watch the street beyond the house, barking loudly if anyone so much as lingers with possible intent along our boundary line. As a reward for being such an excellent security guard, I'm given sneaky treats and taken out for a lovely walk to unwind before my next shift begins."

108

Farley

"Ssshhh, I'm on cat patrol!"

Leon

German Shepherd/Labrador cross   Commissioned by Clare Matthews

"Do you happen to have any toys on you? It's just that I really love playing with toys. I love it when my friends bring their toys to the park and let me 'borrow' them. I'm a bit of a joker so I usually run off with them, hoping they will chase me to get them back. Of course, I always let them have their toys when we leave because I've got plenty of my own at home.

I'm a strong swimmer and love open water swimming for pleasure, though not in competitions or anything like some people do, as I'm a bit too old for that. I like my home comforts too much to do all that training – give me a big comfy bed to lie in and I'm one happy pooch!"

110

Leon

"If you're nipping to the shops I'd like a new ball, please!"

Dolly

Jack Russell

Commissioned by David Blaikie

"I have this older brother called Hodge who has sharp teeth and a bossy side, especially when food is around. It took me quite a while to build up enough confidence to dish out some of his own medicine, and remind him that the pecking order can change!

The brilliant thing is that, now, all I have to do is just stand and stare at him when he's snoozing in bed, and he creeps out to let me get in – pre-warmed and cosy!

I met my Mum and Dad (and Hodge) ten years ago, after wandering up and down Portobello High Street. I wasn't looking for antiques – I was lost. After seven days of wagging my tail waiting for someone to come and claim me, these lovely people (and Hodge) came to get me, saying that they had completely fallen in love with me ... well, maybe not Hodge straight away but soon after ... perhaps."

Dolly

"Sorry ... did you say something ...?"

Florence

Cavapoo   Commissioned by Claire Smith

"A few choice pleasures can make my day special, and most of them include food and eating.

I like riding in the van, going for a woodland walk with a big stick in my mouth, picking wild raspberries and blackberries from the bush, and mixing them with crunchy rabbit poo!

I love laying on cushions having a tummy tickle before falling into a deep sleep beside my Mum. I absolutely hate noise, squeaks and rattles, and detest cartoons on the television and flapping pigeons, claw clipping, and unnecessary grooming.

My biggest bugbear, though, is finding an empty food bowl. How lackadaisical is that ...?"

Florence

"Oooh, yes! A nice cup of tea would be just the thing – with milk and sugar, please!"

Derry

Kelpie

Commissioned by Emma Gamble

" I used to suffer terribly with my nerves when I was adopted as a puppy at seven months old. I've managed to block out most of the trauma of that time, but still remember being terrified of walking down the street: there were so many scary noises, and people, and traffic ...

I hated anyone touching me, which makes me laugh now because I work at the university, training students how to become animal physiotherapists. One of the perks of the job is a full-body massage before my daily romp in the fields.

Whilst I de-stress from my highly responsible job, I can run for hours, totally losing myself in the moment (and often the long grass). I keep meaning to tell someone where I'm going and when I'll be back ... "

Derry

"Go ahead: I'm all ears!"

Bertie

Greyhound Commissioned by Kay Race

"Hello, I'm an ex-racer from Ireland. Life as an athlete was all about running fast and winning the race, but now that I've retired I live in a posh house with carpets and open rooms. No more hard floors and cages for me!

Retirement has brought a new career as a therapy dog. I visit old people with dementia – they smile when they see me, and it doesn't matter that they can't remember things, they're just happy to spend time with me.

As a treat the chef in the home prepares me a slice of ham, and I pop along to the kitchen to collect it before we leave.

We always go by car because I hate the rain and getting wet. I'll even walk around a puddle to avoid getting my feet wet!"

Bertie

"I think the weather forecast said rain later ... I'll stay inside: no point chancing it!"

Lexi

Patterdale   Commissioned by Nicky Hartle

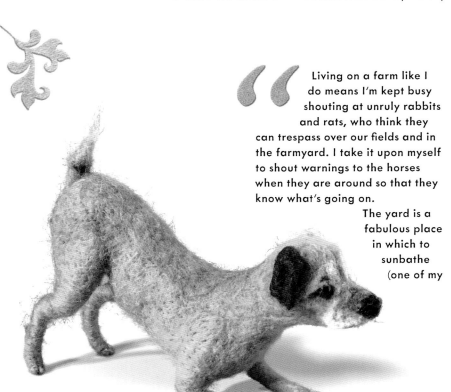

"Living on a farm like I do means I'm kept busy shouting at unruly rabbits and rats, who think they can trespass over our fields and in the farmyard. I take it upon myself to shout warnings to the horses when they are around so that they know what's going on.

The yard is a fabulous place in which to sunbathe (one of my favourite outside pursuits), and one of my favourite indoor pastimes is sleeping under the duvet, preferably with my Dad.

This is also where I hide when idiots are letting off fireworks, I so hate the sudden loud bangs. Another of my pet hates – no pun intended – are other Terriers, I'm the only Terrier who's important around these parts. Others are fake and quite unnecessary!

"On your marks ... get set ... GO!"

Beanie Bear

Jack Russell   Commissioned by Kiaran Black

"Mum often uses me as her lumbar support cushion when she works from home. I'm glad to be of help because she often takes me to the seaside for a paddle or into the woods to run after mice. I also like a good fairytale, and my favourite is *The Princess and the Pea*, which I like to re-enact with cushions piled up on the sofa next to my Dad each evening as I fall asleep in front of the fire. I'm quite an old lady, you see, and suffer from age-related facial hair, which Mum thinks looks brilliant!

I doubt she'll think the same in a few years' time when it happens to her ..."

Beanie Bear

"Here's lookin' at you, kid!"

Jade

Chihuahua   Commissioned by Rosemarie David

"Prized possessions are often small, and I'm one of those small treasures who make people feel blessed in my company ... not that I'm big-headed, or anything! I like other dogs, and am never snappy, even though most of them are over twice my size. I love being held and getting attention, and I give attention in equal measure.

I know that I am handsome because everyone says so, which is nice. I repay their compliments with gentle licks, and an even layer of my hair on their clothes.

One act of kindness deserves another, eh?!"

Jade

"Love often comes in small packages ..."

Willow

Spaniel   Commissioned by Julie Sleight

" When I first joined my family I was a bit scared of the other dog they have, but he's actually quite nice, and I soon found the confidence to drag him about by his collar, and get him to join in with my adventures.

Some of my adventures have resulted in near-death experiences! I once played 'Chicken' with a car and lost, badly breaking my leg, and having to spend weeks recovering, which actually gave me enough time to plan my next adventure – to swim across a raging river! I had to be rescued from that, too, after nearly drowning, so, for the time being, I'm restricted to sunbathing in the garden.

It's a lot safer than real bathing! "

Willow

"It wasn't me, honest, Mum!"

Stephanie's creations

Stephanie's models are based on photographs of pets supplied by her clients, and each model takes a very long time to make. Needle felting involves building up layer upon layer of wool fibres, stabbing them repeatedly, thousands of times, with a single barbed needle, forcing the fibres to knit and 'felt' together.

These models comprise the majority of Stephanie's work, but she also runs school-based workshops, for both adults and children, demonstrating how to make everything from flat felt pictures to three-dimensional felt animals.

For further details of Stephanie's creations and workshops, visit her website:

http://stephaniecowburn.com